Purposeful Pup

Written by
Patric Rayburn

Illustrated by
Sydney Provencher

To all the hands that hold and help them along their way.
—*Patric Rayburn*

To children who's masterpieces live in the margins of notebooks.
—*Sydney Provencher*

Tella Tales LLC
Decatur, Georgia

Cuddly and snuggly,
my little ear blue,
I started out
small with a
big job to do.

With brothers
and sisters, I
played, slept,
and snacked.
But eight short
weeks later,
my cage door
click-clacked.

Into a car I went, then a dark room—
Bound for an airplane that away would zoom.

It was bumpy and loud on my first airplane trip.
I tried to be brave, with a stiff upper lip.

Then the plane stopped; all went quiet and still,
I saw smiling faces; I felt my heart fill.

I have to admit, it was
rough that first night.
No brothers and sisters to
sleep on—what fright!

But up came the sun,
and we went out to play.

My new friend taught me
how to sit and to stay.

I learned new commands
and what "don't" and
"off" meant.
But then things all changed,
and to work we two went.

Although my ears filled
with an ooh-and-aah sound,
I quickly learned I could
not romp around.

Emails and calls and some
long meetings, too.
I couldn't care less, I just
lazed my way through.

Puppy School
Then a new change; I went to puppy school!
They looked like my brothers and sisters—how cool!
IN TRAINING
IN TRAINING

Puppy Sch
IN TRAINING
We practiced walking up and back a lot. Next to my friend became my favorite spot.

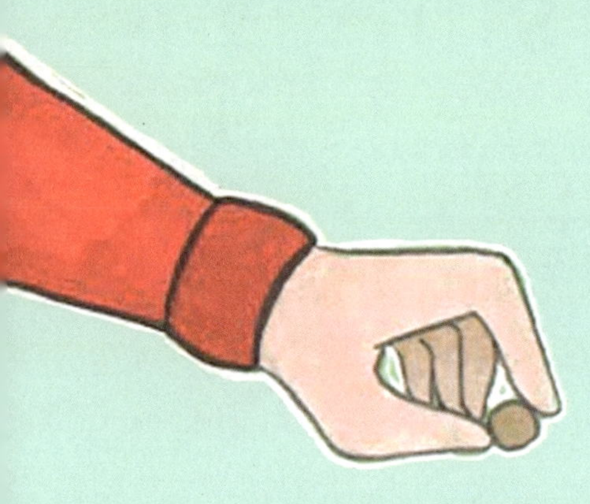

Each thing I learned came with plenty of love—
Sit and stay, of course, and when not to shove.

I learned how to jump, shake,
and even bark, too.

Teaching tools for the
work I'd one day do.

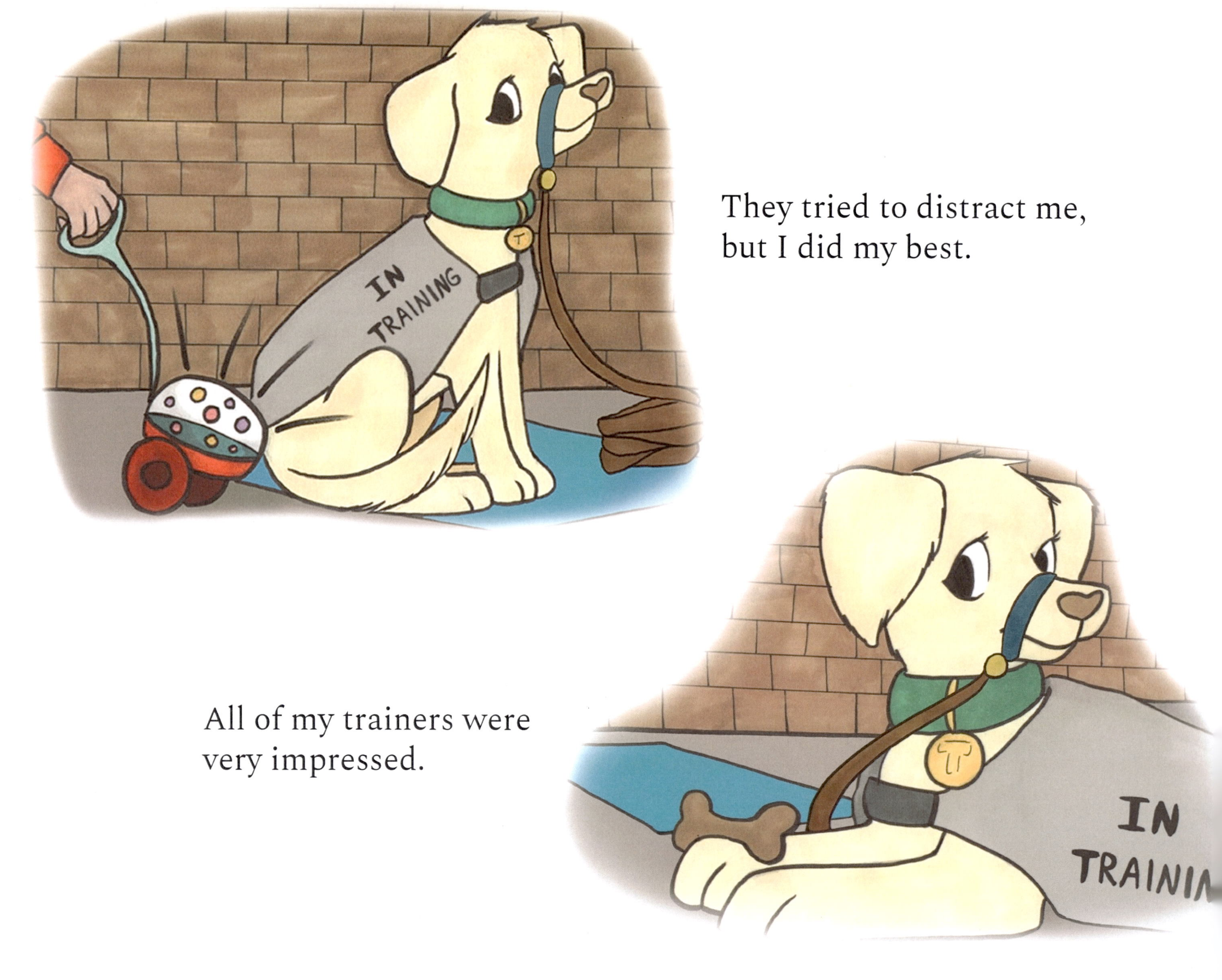

They tried to distract me, but I did my best.

All of my trainers were very impressed.

My friend took me places
that others can't go.

The grocer and barber
I soon got to know.

In no time at all a whole year
had flown by.
My friends were now family,
on whom I relied.

KETCHUP

Then one big day, they took me someplace new.
I stood on a stage, though my friends seemed quite blue.

We hugged and we snugged
and then they walked away.
I didn't know what it all
meant that day.

I soon found out that I had a new crew.
I met new friends who sensed this strange day, too.

Advanced Training
ADVANCED TRAINING
VANCED INING

Class started
fast at this new
puppy school.
No romping
allowed, and
no being
a fool.

Staying in school meant
behaving just right.
Some didn't do well and
soon left our sight.

Six months this went on,
until a boy came.
He looked down at me and
said, "Ian's my name."

He needed help; I knew
just what to do.
I showed him all of the
cool stuff I now knew.

Tugging socks off, getting things off the ground,

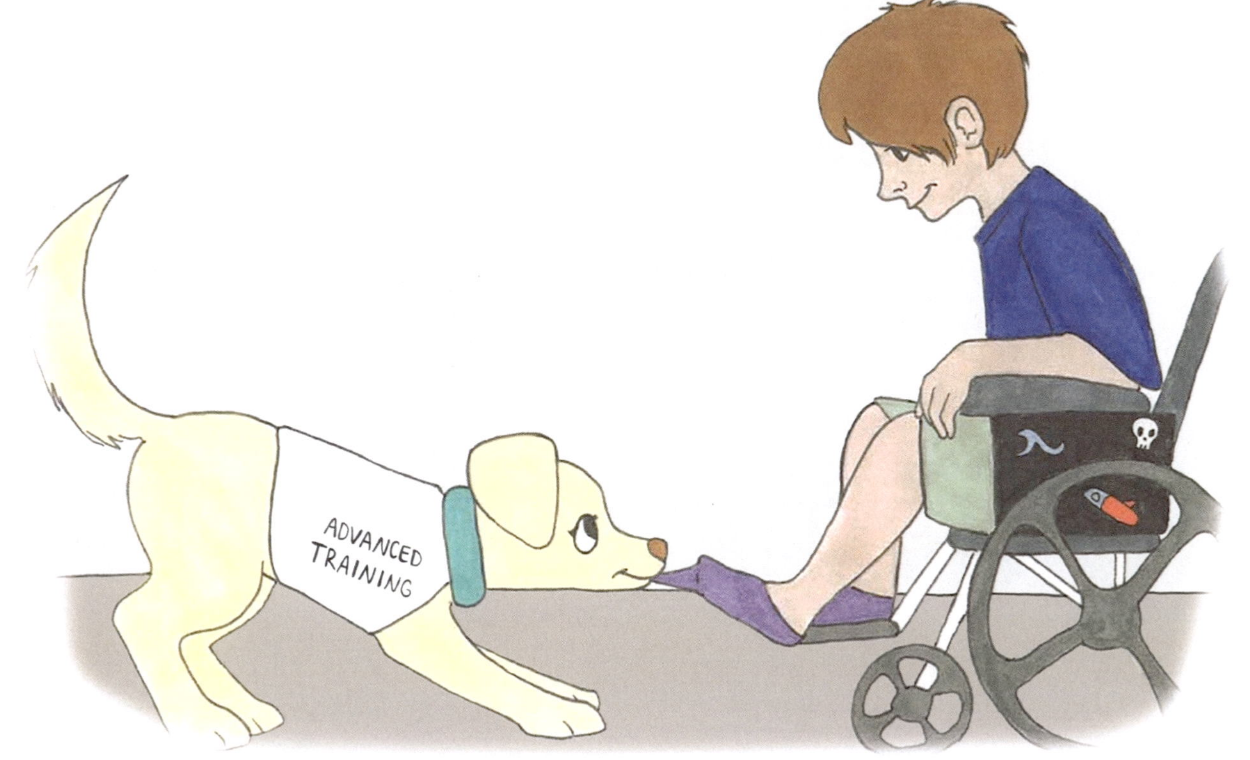

And the comfort I bring whenever I'm around.

Together, we practiced until we were pooped. "A match!" my teacher said; they cheered and they whooped!

The reason for all I had learned was now clear. We'd take on the world together without fear.

My crew dressed me up in
honor of the day.
This time was special, but
why I can't say.

To my surprise, my
friends walked
through the door.
We hugged
and we
snugged,
so happy I
could roar!

Up on the stage, smiling through a big sniffle.

They gave me to Ian and made it official.

We arrived home, both our
feelings so strong,
And I curled up where
I've always belonged.
Welcome Home Tella!

In my heart I'll always hold every day
The hands that held and helped me along my way.

I found my purpose with a cool new crew.
You may be small, but think of all you'll do!

Why was Tella's little ear blue?
Why did her trainers try to distract her?
Why did she learn to bark?

Visit www.PurposefulPup.com to learn more about
these fascinating nuances of training a purposeful pup!

PATRIC RAYBURN is a volunteer trainer of service dogs, also known as a "puppy raiser." The first puppy he and his wife raised is named Tella and she graduated from one of the largest service dog training organizations in the United States and was placed with an amazing boy named Ian. This book is inspired by Tella's journey to Ian. When Patric isn't chasing four-legged friends around, he works in marketing and communication in Atlanta where he lives with his wife, son and their forever-dog Matcha.

 @workingwoof

SYDNEY PROVENCHER is an illustrator and graphic designer who loves all things "art." She adores video games, tattoos, guitars, and horror films and allows those to inspire her work. She currently lives in Michigan with her close family, and couldn't be happier.

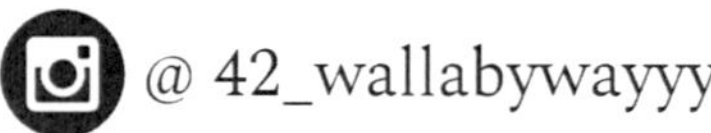 @ 42_wallabywayyy

SPECIAL THANKS TO: Kat Rayburn, Melissa Coleman, Ian, Lauren and Luke McFarland, Mindy Ruiz, Reinert B the Dog, Tami Boyce, Brooke Vitale, Tim Victor, Kim Paquette, and Misty, Doug, and Nolan Provencher.

CPSIA information can be obtained
at www.ICGtesting.com
Printed in the USA
LVRC080912081121
702742LV00004B/58